SCORING IN INJURY TIME

SCORING IN INJURY TIME

Francis Sparshott

Wolsak and Wynn . Toronto

©Francis Sparshott, 2006

No part of this publication may be reproduced, stored in a retrieval system or transmitted, in any form or by any means, without the prior written consent of the publisher or a licence from The Canadian Copyright Licensing Agency (Access Copyright). For an Access Copyright licence, visit www.accesscopyright.ca or call toll free to 1-800-893-5777.

Cover image: Francis Sparshott
Author's photograph: Francis Sparshott
Typeset in Garamond
Printed in Canada by The Coach House Printing Co. Toronto, Ontario

The publishers gratefully acknowledge the support of the Canada Council for the Arts, the Ontario Arts Council, and the Book Publishing Industry Development Program (BPIDP) for their financial assistance.

| Canadian | Patrimoine |
| Heritage | canadien |

The Canada Council for the Arts | Le Conseil des Arts du Canada

Wolsak and Wynn Publishers Ltd
196 Spadina Avenue, Suite 303
Toronto, ON
Canada M5T 2C2

Library and Archives Canada Cataloguing in Publication

Sparshott, Francis, 1926-
    Scoring in injury time / Francis Sparshott

ISBN 1-894987-09-8

I.   Title.
PS8537.P3S36 2006   C811'.54   C2006-900659-8

Acknowledgements

"The poet in a changing world" appeared in *A Vic sort of man*, edited by Mary Love and Hertha Schulze (Toronto, 2001). None of the other poems have appeared before.

This collection of my verse is dedicated to the memory of Kitty, my dear wife for more than half a century. She would have liked the poems to be more cheerful, but these are what I have.

Contents

Road mending 9
Sometimes a few geese 10
Aim and fire 12
Amnesty International writes again 13
Bunting 15
Heron 16
When cormorants came 17
Amaryllis by a winter window 19
The wire walkers 20
Village airfield 22
Beached in Bahamas 23
A patriot's honeymoon 24
Revolution summer 26
Peg o' my heart 27
Old-time religion 28
Evensong: Rochester Cathedral, 1975 29
Los Olvidados 30
Freedom and grace 31
Psalm 23A 33
Cimetière marin 34
Melancthon Cemetery revisited 35
Valedictory observations on Scarborough, Ontario 37
To the mailbox and back 39
At Kingston and Kildonan 40
Thinking it to be the Gardiner 41
Diabolus in musica 42

A long way from Egypt   43
Peter painting Peter Reading   44
The poet in a changing world   47
Borges in translation   50
Heidegger in 1945   51
Pound at Pisa   52
Innisfree lost   53
Poem about a poem about a poem about a rice cake   54
Ludwig Wittgenstein went to war   56
On having once met David Lewis   57
Unqualified success   58
Radicals   59
Scrap books   60
The dam   61
Neither Nausicaa nor Persephone   62
Maidens   63
Danae and Leda   64
The meaning of Hallowe'en   65
An old understanding   66
Ironing day   67
Thinking of Helen Keller   68
You know who I mean   69
To dry   72
A wind dies down   73
Belloc's   74
Christeagle   75
Cooking apples   76
By Rice Lake   78

Road mending

I walk out evenings onto the wide empty road,
filling in crusted potholes, whitening faded signs.
I imagine purposeful traffic
roaring against horizons, detours, hills.

No hoof, no tire, disturbs the bland highway.
We built it back then, but the young people tell me
the pavement was always there, stretched out, divided.
Roads leading Romeward dived under dark seas.

Has somebody somewhere authorized a bypass?
Have cars gone back to their familiar ways
we called the Indian Trail, following contours
around blind corners under visible trees?

Mine is the best way, though I have never seen
what lies at the end. Only incurable love
leads me beyond my gate when shades gather
with my barrow of gravel, my paint for the doubled lines.

Sometimes a few geese

Geese come ashore,
noble, serious, proud,
stalk shattered stone
of our grey beach, stripping
hard seeds from drying grass.
They post their sentinel
to stare us down. This is our property,
we'd say, if he would hear. Once and again
he sounds his quiet tone. Slowly, by ones and twos,
not answering, they plod
back down onto the lake, into their own world,
not caring if we follow.

Sometimes before I sleep
I stand on grey boulders by an unwrinkling water.
My father is there.
He has been speaking to me.
I do not recall his words, if I ever heard them.
He turns and strides back into uncertain air
between water and rock till there is nothing left
for me to see. If geese are flying south
I cannot tell. Their day is gone.
A few bats are busy around dark trees.
Some day I must follow Father. Now my bed calls me
from an uninviting shore.

Sometimes in spring
when snow has drifted and deepened its black season
we return to a risen lake
lapping the tamarack roots of a thrawn bush,
ninebark drowning to death, even the grey willows
stopped in their strength. We are here
on a buckled layer of rock, humped by a lost age
out of the water, taken and overgrown
by birch and cedar. Winters like this,
ice driven and cracked by an onshore gale
shatters the dolomite skins, sliding and grinding
rubble to gravel. One year the lake will fall,
seeds find new shelter among white shales:
gentian, thoroughwort, and a new growth
of willows. Here on an unchanging ground
that is crumbled and piled for ever, we will stand
as we always stood, lords of a broken place
where the geese come ashore.

Aim and fire

Who mostly misses?
The incompetent marksman
with a perfect gun.

Who always misses?
The impeccable marksman
with a crooked gun.

Hit and miss, we say,
being just such as we are
with the arms we have.

Amnesty International writes again

Autumn: while sullen geese
fly crankily south
past migrant raptors
that comb the cliff's bushy rim
where trembling warblers crouch in deciduous
shade, today's mailing brings
my annual update on the world's
torment. A hundred nations –
more than a hundred now, because that world
grows worse, and the sovereign states
divide, each into its own
set of low tribes, detesting, detestable –
police in a hundred lands make torturing
their instrument of policy. More each year:
they learn from each other, purchasing each other's
obsolete arts of pain, taught by retired technicians
from the confession factories of Great Powers,
experts in agony and shame. Places too poor
to feed the citizenry, heal them, house them,
school them, none are too indigent
to build their presidents palaces, bishops basilicas,
buy the gendarmes new guns, new uniforms, fresh tools
to shine and sparkle, spreading brains and blood.
Next year will be different, fashions change
in styles of humiliation; what will not change
is government, the will to tax and torment.

Their torn compatriots with broken hopes
in the dark are strangers to them; to police
all cops are comrades. Pet cats wait in our gardens
by the birds' feeding station. Geese flap south,
mourning and imperturbable. New mail
thuds on the mat: news of the new nations,
each with its own smart force, joining the world's court,
soundproofing cells, with blinds for barred windows.

Bunting

It had flown fast and low
into the chromed trap
of a snarling automobile
to be brusquely hustled aside
on forced migration
where neither mate nor forage
promised a sweet season.

Neck snapped, plumes askew,
blue down grooved and ruffled
by an arbitrary gale,
it hangs while the tires pound
roads paved and gravelled
and squeal for the quarry turn.
Motion comes to an end.

Cherries garnish the hedge
and a scatter of blackeyed susan
springs from the ditch below.
Gently the shamed driver
frees what was drooping there
from the hot ticking grille,
throws it away, drives on.

No one is there to say,
shaken and sad, he has seen
his first indigo bunting,
has borne it for miles on miles,
his car's bright blazon
unnamed, unknown
into sweet summer air.

Heron

A great blue heron
stands by a quiet lagoon,
ventures a creaking
step and is still. Now
it thinks it is a tree –
turtles fumble its root –
green ash, grey willow. It dreams
of small trusting minnows
rubbing their tickly fins
over its ankles. Tourists,
sprouting binoculars, wait
for the stabbing beak. But the bird,
striding and splattering, flaps
out of the misty water
through thickening afternoon
to where old men festooned
with various lenses stand
in a slather of smeared sunblock,
heavy with expectation.

When cormorants came

This year a cormorant joins
shy loons, unheeding gulls,
dark and quiet
squats low in water, riding
a nest of ripples, lifts
hooked beak till it suddenly
dives where fish hide. The ripples,
left to themselves, scatter.
It will break surface somewhere.

Between boat launch and tackle shed
dark and quiet
in an oiled harbour, threading
the tugs' taut hawsers, idle
as thought in a drifting head, she gathers
her shawl of silence round her. Turn,
look back, she's gone, black memory
of who can tell
what paradise, what hell.

Drawn to skill city I drive
as I must, for my life lives there,
stop by last century's mill
to piss and breathe. But the birds
furrow the still pool over the broken dam
together, part, join in remote reed-beds.
Strange seeing cormorants here
quiet and dark
ruling black trails across my sacred places.

I have been home, if home
is where I was young and believed
I would outgrow misery. Last year
I walked again by that salt estuary.
On buoys and bollards they perched and preened
as such fowl will, heraldic, double-crested,
quiet and dark.
There were none when I was a child.
Now they are everywhere, flying fast and low.

Amaryllis by a winter window

Seventeen red
blossoms to crown five
columns of chlorophyll, six
minuscule citrons
shrivelled on small trees
against grey morning.
In a sudden swarm
of sparrows and mourning doves
and the odd chickadee
a surprising hawk
bangs like a gun to leave,
on a shuddering pane, down
from a speckled breast, and a garden
empty of birds and squirrels.
Birds will be back. Tomorrow
sixteen or ten bloodred
blooms broad as a woman's
face – but the rest,
withered and pale, hang
from their gallows. Every day
oranges ripen, rot,
fall off their tiny trees.

The wire walkers

Slung pole to pole between
window and wind, a humming line
hunts green transformers, makes on its way
a street for squirrels straighter than oak branches.
They've devised a special gait for the hydro's bounty,
half stroll, half hop. Once in a while
a squirrel slips. No matter:
it grabs, holds on, makes its way underslung
like a faster sloth. They have learned a new method
for underwire travel. It is all one to them.

Once at my street's high end
where cars come barrelling round
off the highway, hurrying home, I saw a squirrel
dragging inert hindquarters
along the road's edge, nibbling as it went,
lame, busy. Then I saw
one hind leg working still, good for a crawl
but not for hopping, no use for climbing
trees or electric poles. It didn't mind,
it is all one to the wild kingdom,
there is living to be made
grovelling along gutters, doing what can be done
with the legs you have. Now I am pensioned off
it is my life's work to observe the beasts
go by, one way or another.

On this cold morning
old homeless humans woke up to leave
sleeping bags empty on town's busiest corners,
wrote on brown squares
"No job, no hope,
no money; in need of change." I see them soar
into thin sunshine, beating their cardboard wings,
their kapok chrysalis and constraining night
forgotten, changed. It is my job to see
squirrels against grey sky
treading black wires.

Village airfield

They were here tomorrow,
they're here today:
blue plastic hangar
open both ends,
two aircraft tethered
tail to tail –
like paired white admirals
seen one summer
hour after hour
entranced, unmoving
on a forest cedar
engendering others.

On the black apron
private planes
unsheltered, empty,
are parked, pegged.
They are always there
when I drive home
from the local grocer
with bags of eggs,
potatoes, carrots,
daily papers;
wide windy clearing
with aircraft anchored
side by side
or end to end.

Beached in Bahamas

Heard on night's newscast
of cruel killings
and politic sleaze –
beached in Bahamas
a bevy of beaked whales
stink in the sun.

Pinging and pranging,
multiple torment
from massed sonars
of maritime men
herded their hurt
through coralled shallows.

Lying in states
of dissolution
where their gods left them
they head still shoreward,
knowing no need
of reverse gears.

Protean proteins
attend creation
in profound ocean.
What next mutation
awaits selection
for whales in sand?

A patriot's honeymoon

The sturdy chieftain's daughter
married to Stenka Rasin,
to her surprise, was pitched
headlong into the river.
Garland and veil discarded
she tore off her wedding gown,
not to expose the promised
paraphernalia of love
but to kick out better behind
as she swam in his bubbling wake.

So Stenka Rasin remained
loyal to his Cossack crew
as his bride's enraged yells
receded into legend.
On my old scratched LP
a Russian chorus chants
through the hisses and clicks of time
the fame of that murderous drunk,
bridegroom, brigand, hero –
a man's man to the end.

No lasting rumour recalls
how the girl made it to shore,
married a local laird
or reliable real estate,
raised a responsible brood
of solid burgesses, bearing
unmemorable names,
but ready to batter the balls
of tipsy celebrities
like that bastard who married Mum.

Revolution summer

Dazed tricoteuses
with sweaty needles
drop half their stitches;

official bunting
droops from its rigging
too damp to flap;

aristos drop off
under the guillotine
drowsy with death.

Peg o' my heart

My wavering hasty hand
wrote farriery, my dimmed
unspectacled eye next morning
read family. Broken hoops
of iron, slotted for nails,
clanged on the planted peg,
twisting judiciously through the afternoon
from an old hand. If it closes
round me, he's won. Go, grandfather,
play with your pals
at the new casino, pulling
the sweaty levers, making symbols whirr
behind lit windows, till your pension pours
down thirsty slots. Meanwhile, take from my neck
your horseshoes, lucky horseshoes
heated and hardened by a lost trade.

Old-time religion

My mother's a witch;
she has her spells.
Her barbecue burns
under her steaks.

Crocodile shrines
stifle in sand
under the tracks
of Tebtunis trams.

Crocodile mummies
lie cheek by jowl
swathed in papyrus
from tax returns.

Sappho's lost odes
and pagan prayers
are swaddling shrouds
for saurian gods.

My mother's mind
is wide as her smile:
it opens to greet
her savage past.

Evensong: Rochester Cathedral, 1975

Just where the Magnificat
sings *he hath scattered the proud*
the floor of the south transept
blew up in a tile fountain,
sent the chairs flying. Neither soul
nor body was hurt – no miracle;
weekday services draw
no worshippers. But the priest,
hearing two thunderous cracks
and watching his floor dissolve
in a shower of polychrome shards,
thought as his chant went on
in the imagination of their hearts:
"Here comes my martyrdom:
this cruddy edifice,
once Late Perpendicular,
turns horizontal." Wrong!
It was only encaustic tile
expanding and overheating
over excessive light
brought in for a TV shooting
in the old crypt below.
It must be hell down there.

Los Olvidados

Los Olvidados. Wasn't that the name
of a film I dreamed in my heart? In a Castilian
noon of dry torment, among twisted trees
of a dark plantation, ripened fruit falling
into oblivion? When will I learn better?
I still remember, when I am asleep,
a garden on a hillside, swords and torches,
that film I never saw, and a young saviour weeping
in the olive orchard, none of them forgotten.

Freedom and grace

Militant Molinists,
brazen Bañezians,
turn the flame down
under old debates.

Blue jays and mourning-doves
share with black squirrels
our spilled bounty
of millet and maize.
In our young lilacs
juncos and chickadees
attend the feeder.

All is so quiet
baffled Bañezians,
mollified Molinists
stop stupid squabbles.

In morning sunlight
benches drowse
as kids cram classrooms
and pensioned parents
around scrubbed tables
caress cold coffees.

The park prepares
for noontime nannies
and matrons minding
doggy business.
Under this cloud
the Sudbury plane
grinds in the offing
its friendly grumble.

East over ocean
under damp beeches
in a town garden
stands a bench bearing
my parents' names
and the days they died.

Boys with new knives
effaced one Sunday
that sad reminder.
Municipal seating
in clammy climates
needs constant care.

Bañezians, bury
your tarnished tomahawks;
Molinists, sheathe
your needling pens.
The Sudbury plane
purrs through the mist
where grace meets freedom.

Psalm 23A

The Lord was my shepherd
I lacked something
his rod and staff
woke me and prodded me
out of green pastures
shearing my fleece
fanks a lot
he led me up into the diesel transport
idleness and mercy
following far behind
I felt nothing
surely I'll hang my head
in the Lord's freezer
for ever and after

Cimetière marin

A famous bone yard by the central sea:
white doves over the blue tiles sailed
cooing and crawling
into anthologies. Now colder air
is yellow and thick between new tenements.
Bereaved bourgeois slam
doors of occasional cabs, bring to stone slabs
their vinyl posies of remembrance.
That cemetery closed, crammed with the dead,
the poet's vista sundered from his shore
by tanks, tubes, gantries of refineries
mixing and cooking, stinking and pumping, keeping
fragile economies
afloat. The wind is rising, ruffles
plastic petals. Better leave now and make
another stab at life.

Melanchthon Cemetery revisited

Is this your graveyard?
Most of the stick-on
letters have gone
from the sign. Small seedlings –

pine, maple, juniper –
jut and crawl
around and over
honey-cold carven

stones with their dates of death
crumbled and fallen
like stuck-on script
from neglected boards.

Mementoes cluster
on a grassed knoll
where Highway Ten
comes curving round

with its doubled line:
tilted tablets
and sturdy scrub
between. But the green grass grows
round all. The nearest farmer,
riding his red machine
Saturdays, whirs and clatters,
mowing it close.

Melanchthon Cemetery,
where are your dead?
When they shifted your stones
to straighten their road,

whose yellow engines
scattered and lost
the mashed remains
of pioneers?

Valedictory observations on Scarborough, Ontario

I came to my town in young zeal,
settled in the south where cliffs crumbled.
Pheasants and gold foxes
shrieked and scrambled
over the clay; bank swallows
burrowed blown sand each June, called to each other
their news of nesting. Now I am past work
I sit by the cliff edge while day strengthens
watching the redwings flash their bright shoulders.
The foxes are gone, the pheasants and the swallows.
Distant and silent on the benign waters
two freighters making for their next harbour
wait out the weekend as their world goes nowhere.
Sunday yacht masters spread deceptive sails
to a light breeze, masking the prudent purpose
of pumping power. Sabbath skies
are full of voices: constant trundle of planes
that shadow the shoreline, sometimes the deep groan
of a liner heading for its island field
and, once, gruff gunfire
of a helicopter bustling its grim freight
of cops or journalists to report or rescue.
Below them, headlong, close to the lake surface,
thin skeins of geese are sketching different trails
to preferred pastures. From lilacs and tall maples
all round come calls and carols of hidden birds,
some that I know – cardinal, dove, phoebe –

more that I can't remember, many and many
I'll never learn. At the next bench over
a small child is wailing, as a baby cries,
for no known reason. Looking up, I see
those freighters have crossed paths. So they were moving.
Things change. The sun gets higher, and the wind
subsides. Last year, provincial power decreed
the town where I came to live does not exist,
we are all the big city now. I see a man
down there in a rowboat moving along the beach:
rocks where he passes show as black shadows
under the still surface. I'll go indoors,
lunch, write this down, wind up the tall clock.

To the mailbox and back

Trees you once planted shut out the sky.
Foolishness hides heaven.
Write letters to friends
while they can still see.
Send taxes to this official
or that; let them take counsel
whether to spend them. Lick
bright stamps, take on your tongue
that sharp familiar savour
of government gum, like the French kiss
of a dead clerk. Press well down
or edges will curl and slide.

Now take your tremulous sendings
slowly to mail. In the savage city
white trucks will venture, clearing red boxes
any time now. Walk home
between those trees you planted as a young man
against bitter blizzards and the sharp eyes
of rowdy children with their chattering nannies
shutting out the sky.

At Kingston and Kildonan

Remember Ma's Lunch
where dallying drivers
left gold bulbs winking
and dived indoors
on lawless breaks
while marooned riders
with words to be kept
made patient pretence
of unfelt warmth?

They pulled that down,
piled in its place
a cheesy flatblock
where coffee is decaff
freeze-dried, quaffed
at tinny tables.
Disconsolate buses
go round and round.
It wasn't great coffee
but it was coffee
at Ma's Lunch.

Thinking it to be the Gardiner

Creepers and rust cascade
from this crisp tip
where an unfinishable street
leans on its concrete trestle. In crannies
of subway stairs, besieging banks and chapels,
cresses and dandelions
scramble toward dark clouds; soft rain
runs her caressing hands
under my collar, heads for the rolling hills
at the base of my spine.
Is this Cathay wrapped in its fragrant fable
of robes and bureaucrats
embroidering banished garrisons
with plaintive prosody, while guards
hack thick throats
of surly peasantry (*sullen, refractory,
cut down in the melting snow*) in spurting red
calligraphy? No, it is only spring
in my own town, where buds
rejoice in grime
under last winter's nails.

Diabolus in musica
[on a poem by Carole Satyamurti]

"A Devil in Music" – the fraught verse
is signed with a star. Fallen,
it creeps under foot, low note: weatherworn tritone
among the strums. "Men of the muddle ages
deemed it distasteful, cee to eff sharp." Masters
of heavenly harmony, universal frame
discarding discord? No. It was the Devil
in dark person, accusing
the brethren, slap
in the octave's face, stuck halfway, going
nowhere, irresolute, doggedly unmodish,
lockjaw without key, jarring, ajar
in a filthy temper.

A long way from Egypt
[On "Rest on the flight into Egypt," a poem by
A.F. Moritz after a painting by Bernard van Orley]

Late in his chilled summer a poet sees
a woman with a sleeping child. The painter
saw no such thing, only a sturdy chap
upright and wide awake, climbing the crimson cliff
of an opulent skirt, his right foot plantigrade,
the left leg braced, toes springing, clammy lips
mumbling the offered teat, ten fingers spread
over naked flesh, round eyes intent
on a gold medallion barely out of reach
round Mother's neck. She looks down, calculating
how long this meal will take. She takes no notice
of clambering legs, of reaching hands. One arm
supports a wriggling rump, one arm enfolds
a thrusting shoulder. Meanwhile a thick book
lies by her sandalled foot. She cannot read
but will look carefully, once her infant sleeps,
at the illustrations. See how the careful painter
laboured on this illuminated page
for her to look at when the gallery's closed.
Which way to Egypt? There is no ring of gold
over the sacred head, but on Mother's face
that cool considering smile, and, hemming her red robe,
long yards of tarnished braid.

Peter painting Peter Reading

Slumped on his paperback,
bardically glowering, jersey
and jeans smeared
with carefully tactile paint,
in his hand a tottering
beaker of plonk – symbol
of metrics skewed
by postmodern sensibility –
big round eyes (all the better
to imagine you, my dear) conscientiously
scowl at his painting friend
from under their simian ridge. We appear
not to have shaved this morning
or yesterday: nothing like stubble
to strengthen a jawline. Comb the hair forward, Pete,
and muss it a little . . . there. But those baby blues!
Where did he ever get them?

– From the painter's pattern book,
Liverpudlian edition. That's how we do
the vision of genius, German romantic version,
Nietzsche especially, and old silent
films. It's a joke: look at the scratches sketched
on the stones behind him: hand,
crayfish or lobster – and, nudging his drink,
what should be an ammonite but isn't really:
an uncoiled watch spring. The poet is interrupted –
which explains the surly glare – in the important act
of scratching his groin. Like a gentleman,
he was using his left hand.

He's been looking, he tells his readers,
at a sepia portrait of greatgrandad, staring
at life with that bland complacency
Victorians showed, indifferent or blind
to the imminent fall of empire.

Peter! That's how they looked. Like you,
they were having their pictures taken.
It was the long exposures. What we see
is the strain of keeping one's head
unwavering, eyes unblinking. Iron forks,
padded with velvet, hold
the neck firm. They are not thinking
of empire or anything much except
not fidgeting. And the cost. But all those others –
the ruined negatives,
where they twitched and trembled
or sneezed, far from complacent –
grandchildren don't see those, the glass recoated
or scrapped. Yet, smearing or blurred,
they were taken, paid in advance:
eminently Victorian. Lucky young poet,
not needing to hold still
for the other Peter, who knows
how to do poets' eyes.

Between the beetling brows and the sagging pouches
he dabs them in, while the poet
unwinds, straightens his glass,
drains it,
and gets back to scratching his balls.

[Note: the painting of Peter Reading by Peter Edwards is on the cover of the former's *Collected Poems I: Poems 1970-1984*. The poem referred to is "Stills," on page 38 of that book.]

The poet in a changing world
[Panel discussion, League of Canadian Poets, Edmonton 1972]

The first poet:

What is the poet's position?
    Should he be upright?
    (If so, should he be supported?
       Universities actually have chairs)
      need he know Hungarian?
        – one could talk more about the Dutch situation
      there is fellowship at Leeds
         (there are a number of dangers)
regions that support poets are supported on shoestrings.

The second poet:

Australia and Eire are unfashionable places
the best things happened when there was no money
Baxter is a New Zealander and nearly great
I went to my father's town for the smell of hay
    cow pats and so forth
  but there was a bardic festival
      and I felt that everything was coming together.

The third poet.

That we are unknown is our own fault
we should move round the world as writers because we are
                                                             writers
I went to the bookstore in Ibadan –
   Leonard Cohen was there in US editions
I made a snail's track round the immense globe
you can get a thousand bucks without too much difficulty
I am better known than some other Canadians
if the first audience likes your stuff it will snowball
the scene is immediate
there are twenty groups in the immense maze of London
it's all possible
write to people in their own countries
buy your own books and send them out
   spend money on postage
they are morbidly fascinated
       to find poetry written in Canada

I came against total blank walls in external affairs
you can be damned good and not known
that is the way I think about myself
get out beyond the artificial shell
      the bardic thing if you like
          the travelling bard.

The fourth poet (from the floor):

I find it very bothering
to find myself among a lot of businessmen
I hoped to be among my peers
I can meet businessmen anywhere else
this really bothers me.

Borges in translation

There dwelt a poet in ancient Argentina:
I found his poems in a sombre binding
with my own language on the facing page.
I have no Spanish, but my head turned
to see what the English meant. I kept reading
the same words over: dream, Buenos Aires,
sunset and dawn, moon, mirror, oblivion,
death, Heraclitus, Borges, Buenos Aires.
I marvel at the courtesy of Spaniards
who let you know when there will be a question
with a curled sign before they start asking.
Authors in my unceremonious nation
of the brutish North will never let on,
until the question's over, that they've asked one.
Why did the blind librarian in my book
speak of his love for Saxon lands and lore?
He says he doesn't know. In Buenos Aires
the sun moves over the wrong side of the sky.

Heidegger in 1945

In the forgetfulness of being
in the darkening of truth
in the space of a cancelled chair
and a denied pension
he broods in a sacred hut
on the cold summer hills.
He hears from beyond the foot
of the rough wooden stair
a rumour of life stirring –
rat, burglar, Jewish professor.
Heidegger keeps no cat.
Heidegger walks no dog.
Heidegger's sons are lost in the war.
Heidegger reaches out for a candle.
The last matchbox is empty.
He creeps down into gloom
but after the last step
is another step. He falls
in forgetfulness of being.
Time takes his bloody nose
into her black forest.

Pound at Pisa

Wavering wit, woven
of clear light and scalding
tears under damp awning,
wars done with, peers
back to a milder sun
warming brash bards
in courtyards and coffee houses
further than Idaho.

In his brain's narrowing beam
they are closing the best cafés,
jailing the German waiters –
thirty years back. The light
leans as it always leaned
over the prison, stands
like a tower of spilled stone
where Benito fell.

Innisfree lost

Yeats in his Irish autumn
casts off with a girl,
oar thrust through rowlock, looks
for his lake isle at last.

It is lost in short chop and sharp
gusts. He is never to find it,
nary a bee or bean, rows
back to his jetty, decants
a chilled colleen.

He hears in his deepening heart
talkative conclaves, rhymers and senators
over grey sidewalks, up the steep
carpeted stairs.

Poem about a poem about a poem about a rice cake

Dogen heard the old saying: a painted rice cake
does not satisfy hunger. Dogen replied:
"The paints for painting rice cakes are the same
as for painting hills and rivers. They are real,
perfectly good paint. If you say
the painting is not real
you say the phenomenal world
is not real. The entire universe
is a painting, the empty sky
nothing but a painting. *Since this is so,*
there is no help for it, nothing
will satisfy hunger other
than a painted rice cake.
Without painted hunger
you will not be a true person."

Aristotle in the sleep of death
woke to the words "this is so."
"A painted rice cake," he yawned, "is real,
painted with real paints by a real painter.
If you want to eat paintings,
go ahead, eat the painting. You'll still be hungry.
Count yourself lucky if it's painted on rice paper.
You are a true person. If you were a painting
you could not say the empty sky
was a painting, or if you did
the world would not hear you with its painted ears."

Dogen did not hear Aristotle
from his sleep of death. He had finished his commentary,
called to his servant: "Boy!
Fetch me my nosh! I have been working all day,
I am really hungry." "Sorry, master, can't help you.
There is nothing left in the larder
but rice cake."

Ludwig Wittgenstein went to war

The fate of our discipline
said Bertie the third Earl
hangs on young Ludwig. We believe
the next great advance will be his. . . . In a slow boat
on the Vistula, Ludwig was driven
downstream with his rough crew,
refining the basis of logic
in his leisure hours. All night
he was manning a searchlight, amid the remains
of a mishandled army that stumbled and died
on the way back to Cracow. In Cracow the poet Trakl
wrote from his mental hospital, pleading
for letters and talk. When the boat
made landfall at last, it was too late
for visiting hours. In the morning
they told him the mad poet
took poison two days ago.
How sad, Ludwig told his diary.
He had his own room at last. The basis of logic
can never be told, he knew;
it is unspeakable. But it can be shown.

On having once met David Lewis

Counterproductive
they tell me
counterintuitive
in a mist
counterfactual
possible worlds
uncountable
worlds of if only
worlds of my mother's arms
worlds of my summer outings
gone too
worlds of school mornings
gone thank the Lord
(if only
if the Lord would only exist)
of my hopeful season
gone
of my peaceful heart
they are all possible
worlds they are every
world except this
world where I am
that is present to me
that is all
that's all the difference
I am all and nothing
to my dear, dread, only
impossible world.

Unqualified success

My Québec colleague
wrote French poems,
took them to Paris.
An editor said:
"Remove the adjectives."
His book came out
epithet-free.
It won no prizes
but readers relished
how he made margins.
Back home from France
he told his tale,
gave his advice:
"Take them all out."
I never knew
I'd written so many.
They're all gone now.
I lined them up
at the foot of the page.
Verse is a lattice
of sounds and spaces.
Maybe tomorrow
I'll put them back.

Radicals

The Chinese radical
stands on the left, receiving
one to a dozen strokes
on the right side, to impart
specific sense. On occasion
the radical is on top, or all around,
or beneath. It can stand alone,
filling the whole square;
it has its own meaning then.

Chinese children, asprawl
in streets, write in the dust
two thousand ideograms, learning
long forms and short, no need
for more than a few score
radicals. It is so easy,
once you know how, to inscribe
thoughts on your tongue. In the west
we can't do that. None of us know
what radicals are for.

Scrap books

Books grey with grime
bound in stiff buckram, leaning on high
shelves in no order, crammed
with lucid images, sketches, maps, clippings
glued to thick pages
browning and brittle. Not now.
Thick tomes too hefty, worn steps, shaking stools
frustrate my reach. Loose papers wait
unsorted at my side, ready
to fade unfiled. You tall inheritors,
what if you haul
fat folios down, open a few to see
what's saved and stored there, scan crabbed palimpsests
eaten by acid, dare to conjecture
recto and verso turned to oblivion
and a faint trace of stains left too long?
Some still bright leaf
waits in the darkness. Never believe
you will find it. Let it be landfill. Let
new visions shine,
bind them in buckram,
lift them to high
places, leave them in order, while
your knees are strong. My dust
is ready for them.

The dam

Where do words go
Out of a book's body?
Swept in by lens and retina, sent
up seen-it-all stares,
they are lost in looped labyrinths.
No surprised synapse
takes anywhere hold.

These were the light and labour
of notable souls, women
younger than me, mouthing
looks and deep feels
of boiled coffee, kids, deaths,
caresses. Vocables turn
corners and can't find them.

Words that have leapt to the eye fall
back in rough torrents.
Beyond the unladdered shale
meaning in dark pools
waits, ready for spawning,
and a remembered stream
nibbles cold stone.

Neither Nausicaa nor Persephone

I have forgotten the name of Odysseus' wife,
the one who wove and wept. But that's all right.
He stayed with his sea-poppet in her fragrant islet,
that much-enduring, many-minded shit.
But who is the scoundrel bending the big bow,
skewering boyfriends, fooling the dying hound,
conning the doddering dad on his dry hillside?
Owl-eyed Athena had her own reasons
to smooth out wrinkles, crimp the refurbished mane.
Who was that claiming the drowned hero's land?
Only the women knew, and they weren't telling.

Maidens

I have read of maidens in romances.
They were in short supply,
indented for in advance, to be sacrificed
naked to the barley god, buried bloodless
in peat banks on an empty stomach, gagged
and walled in buttresses of fat new
cathedrals. I saw one in a picture
shackled to a seacliff, scaled dragon at heel
winged, taloned, gaping – but that open maw
crammed with the steel spearhead of a bloke perched
on a hippogriff shiny as a blackbeetle.
That was a maiden, neither haired nor slotted
between clamped legs, her blank blancmange of face
upturned to the hero's gaze. He wasn't looking at her,
just at the skewered lizard whose irritation
was fading out to resentful oblivion. But she
looked up at him, not in appreciation
or love or alarm, nor in a snit
at the interruption of her interesting
 rendezvous, but plainly wondering
"What's going on here?" That was the kind of thought
maidens would have. If they were naked they stayed
nuder than needles; once dressed, they remained
dolled up, wrapped to withstand
necessary handling. But there are none left,
no maidens on the shelf, just girls
in deadly armour of "Get lost!", "Get a life!",
"Drop dead!" It crackles round them
like a magnetic storm.

Danae and Leda

What do gods see in us?

Godmaster Zeus paid court to a mortal
girl as a shower of gold.
Was he wearing a safe? Did he become ingot
in the moment's heat? What could have been the point?
Did he want to stand and be counted
time and again
by the hot sticky paws
of an avaricious woman
inflating the currency?

Can you believe a woman
was turned on by a swan?
Nasty bad-tempered critters
with flat flappy webs
between sharp toes on the end
of bony black shins to enfold
the beloved in dank embrace
and narrow yellowy lips
for a horny nibbling kiss. . . .

Did Europa say to her bull
"Don't have a cow, man"?

What do we see in gods?

The meaning of Hallowe'en

Imperious fistlets bang
on a door with a shrill
outcry. A man shuffles
in felt slippers, unlocks,
unbolts, unchains. A light
burns on his porch. On the threshold
a fine figure of a young
woman, busty and blonde,
masked as a crone, recalling
nights on the rainy cusp
of dim Novembers, clutching
in both red hands a white
pillowcase, cannot believe
she is too old for this, mouthing
her "trick or treat." The man
dare not say "trick," stands silent,
opens his fist instead,
letting a few wrapped candies,
left after last year, drool
between fingers, watches them fall
into the soiled bag. It is half empty.
He has nothing more to give. It is half full,
she turns away, says "Happy Hallowe'en,"
carries her careless bosom and cheap sweeties
into the dark street where the next old man
unwraps his hopeless heart.

An old understanding

I know we were young together, I hardly know
how we first met – in a bar? at the church door?
Our eyes caught fire. She ruffled
the short back and sides
of my curled mind. I caressed
her comfy bum. My zip melted away
under her fingers. We meet less often now,
and for a consideration. I have forgotten
Her right name. Was it Melpomene?
Or was that one of her sisters? She calls me "sir"
sometimes, or "dearest." I respond with "Ms"
or "honeybun." Now she is getting on
I'd pay her less; except, now I'm old too,
she'd charge me more. Once, we asked people in
for drinks and conversation; now, it's enough
to sit side by side, her place or mine,
nothing to say all night, thinking how well
we understand each other.

Ironing day

God spits on her iron: a crackle, a dancing bubble,
a brief invisible wisp, nothing. It's hot enough.
God who is satisfied by your dance of death
can settle down now to her serious work
of flattening out the world.
                                        Did you suppose
you would be welcomed at the gates of the sky,
smothered in white feathers? God spits again.

Thinking of Helen Keller

A winged lady, hands reaching out,
wooden skirt flying, carved on a distant island
to be serene and silent, hangs from a screw
on a fine filament. Very slowly
she turns in this quiet air and offers
incomparable blessings; she is more beautiful
than we can understand. What artisan, what god
conspired to open blurred eyes, dying minds
so wide, so deep? She is still turning,
faces me for a while
in the unique mercy of the grace
her maker gave her, then she turns away.

I have known her many years. Days, weeks,
months at a time she hovers there unnoticed,
courtesy wasted on forgetfulness.
Who whittled her, where, when? Is he living still?
Age may have taken him, or the brutal wars,
bullies, gendarmes, beasts, bacteria,
fates that I cannot guess. Did he imagine
somewhere in some cold land an old teacher
would praise his handiwork? No, he made many such
for foreign trade, his living. . . . She has turned away
towards the window. What will become of her
when I too turn away, for the last time?
No one will see her paint fading and flaking,
her body fallen from a snapped thread
to be broken, sold, discarded
in the obliterating avalanche
of tumbling time.

Flavour and scent abandon old heads;
we cannot walk far into fragrant woods.
So much has failed me, but eyes and ears
are loyal still. When they are gone
no painted presence will turn to offer
the visible energy of yearning arms
to bless our helplessness. Will my love stay
to feel, like a blind child,
cold water poured over my hand?

You know who I mean

What was his name? Great
in the convoluted conventional
annals of postmodern
dance in the States, I saw him
dancing or not dancing, late
in his life, in a train station
on a ramshackle trestle. He clambered
to make his entrance, leaned
on a straight chair, with dignity
and caution. All his young dancers
made their own motions round him, a tall
elderly master with a closed
countenance. Did we stand,
or sit on the gritty ground
of Manhattan? So much has gone
with his name. Music was played
I suppose. My mind is building
its own wall round me, the world
keeps crumbling into mumble. But the name
will escape some morning, as names do. Meanwhile
I sit in the living room
of my family home, and the men
come once in a while for the heavy
chairs. They will leave me soon
in an empty place, on a dusty floor,
the parquet scratched where the more awkward pieces
were dragged, among the unfaded oblongs
where pictures hung, carefully chosen

and paid for once, but I don't remember now
what, why, when. One day I'll wonder
where the kitchen is, and if I find the door
how shall I ever turn
the bright white handle? Only a tall dancer,
face lined, illustrious name
eroded, leans on a chair
watching his dancers move.

To dry

Hang these in the sun;
they are old and thoroughly faded,
what tint they had gone to a faint shadow,
a hint of form. I bought them abroad
for bold pattern and bellowing
hues. I have had them so long,
washed them so often, rinsed them, wrung them between
strong hands. . . . Now they are clean again.
Hang them out in the sun.

A wind dies down

In this light air
through my glass pane that could use cleaning
the lowest needles of that spruce I planted
with my gloved hand, decades ego,
are barely stirring. Beyond,
over the road, a Manitoba maple
is in full swing. Breezes sway slim stems,
fuss fanning leaves.

Now the wind dies. My spruce
stands in its sunlight
unshaken. Municipal maples
remain, as it were,
dancing. I cap my pen
carefully, lest the ink dry
over its ball. Always there will be something,
something in motion. I am past seventy.
I must be ready.

Belloc's
[A recantation of Hilaire Belloc's poem "His own country."]

I have come with no companion
but the passport in my hand;
I have said to many people
things they could not understand –
but now I've come to my own country.
It is an altered land.

The trees that grew in my own country
have been cut down and sold.
Most have turned to timber,
bur some to mould.
Every month in my own country
all the woods look old.

Now I've come to my own country
I will crouch down and hide;
I can't find the street I lived on,
long though I've tried.
I have dreamed for seventy years
a sweet dream that lied.

Christeagle

Christeagle
nailed to his gale
hovers, balances,
stoops over unhidden
harmless peckers of grain.
Under my sound roof,
arms outstretched in the dark,
my right rests on the sweat
of a churning fridge and my left
gropes for a chair. Ahead
is unfathomed night:
kitchen, scullery, steps.
Storm of the Christeagle:
credo, talons, beak.

Cooking apples

Oh I forgot to tell you –
on my long journey home
in the soft light that followed
autumn's first shower, I saw
that apple tree by the collapsed
barn that in all these years
has sprawled, meagrely fruited,
split open, spoiled,
shedding its scabbed load
to rot among weeds, like many
in this abandoned land,
lost on the vague margins
of yesterday's orchards, where failed
farmers despaired of soil. In the misty
sunlight I saw it shining
for once, strong-boughed and heavy
with a plump red burden
of food. As I drove on down
I noted at every turning
trees I had never seen
crammed with ripe crimson, in light
I knew for the first time
as *gloaming*. So I perceived
I had toiled a long life away
in a country of apple trees
waiting, by broken barns,
stone piles and snake fences,
to be seen in a better season

and gentler light. But – oh,
I forgot to tell you – in a pasture
where the road swings south, there were two,
two only, heavily brightened
but green. My mother would call them
cooking apples. Something to notice
on the drive home, something to see
by quiet trails, something to remember
after mild sunset, after the first rain.

By Rice Lake

They buried their child
in dirt, under a low mound
by the river, and left. Years turned
as the years will, a thousand, a thousand more
went quietly by, and the river
kept quiet, munching shore
till its mild appetite came
where the child kept her cradle.
On the beach one morning I found
a fine fingerbone, kept it
in a drawer with the sealing wax
and pointless pencils. I've lost
my work and emptied my desk.
It is still there in the dark,
one end blackened with ink
from a leaking ballpoint. Come,
dear heart, it is late
to reach your hand up for my own to hold.
There is only a stained
bone. It is all we have.
I will sit at my desk and warm
what is left of your hand in mine.